St. Paul's Anglican Churchyard S - T

The Grave Whisperer

Angeline Gallant

Published by Angeline Gallant, 2022.

While every precaution has been taken in the preparation of this book, the publisher assumes no responsibility for errors or omissions, or for damages resulting from the use of the information contained herein.

ST. PAUL'S ANGLICAN CHURCHYARD S - T

First edition. September 16, 2022.

Copyright © 2022 Angeline Gallant.

ISBN: 979-8215967669

Written by Angeline Gallant.

Also by Angeline Gallant

A Dragon's Diary
Dreaming of Dragons

Blood and Spirit Saga
The Rising Wind

Calling Her Heart
Whisper of the Heart
Calling Her Heart Volumes 1 & 2: A Small Town Romance
Collection
No Turning Back
Calling Her Heart volumes 3 & 4
Forsake Me Not
Hear My Cry

FORGET ME NOT
Victoria, Ontario's Babies 1894 - 1895

Guardian of the Heart
Fallen Petals

Keeper Of Secrets
A Lady's Secret

Kingston's Love Chronicles
Springtime Promises

Midnight's Awakening
Heart of the Storm
Walking Through The Storm
Walking Through The Storm
Fighting the Storm
Call Me Cursed
Heart of the Storm

Secrets of the Underworld
Deklan's Dragons

Tell My Story Collection
Tell My Story: Germany 1851
Tell My Story: England 1852

Whispers From The Garrison Church

The Dervock Legacy
Echoes of Dervock

The Grave Whisperer
German Prisoners of War in Canada
Cataraqui United Church Cemetery
Whispers of Kingston
Wedding Bells in Kingston, Ontario, Canada 1923
St. Paul's Anglican Churchyard A-B
St. Paul's Anglican Churchyard C-D
St. Paul's Anglican Churchyard E - F
St. Paul's Anglican Churchyard G - H
St. Paul's Anglican Churchyard J - N
St. Paul's Anglican Churchyard O - R
St. Paul's Anglican Churchyard S - T
St. Paul's Anglican Churchyard, Kingston, Ontario T - Z
Small Graveyards & Burial Grounds: Kingston, Ontario, Canada
Cataraqui United Church Cemetery 1
Cataraqui United Church Cemetery 2
Cataraqui United Church Cemetary 3
Cataraqui United Church Cemetery 4
Cataraqui United Church Cemetery 5
Beth Israel Cemetery
Cataraqui United Church Cemetery 6
Beneath the Surface: Echoes from Beth Israel Cemetery
Grave Tales: Discovering the Lives of Beth Israel
Whispers Beneath St. Paul's

The Timeless Veil
Eternal Devotion

The Wolf Whisperer Series
Captured Heart
Fate's Legacy
Mohawk Valley
Cry of a Warrior
Wolf Whisperer volumes 1 & 2
Endless White
The Wolf Whisperer volumes 1 & 2

Timeless
The Time Keeper's Sanctuary

Timeless Whispers of Dervock Saga
Secrets of Dervock

Standalone
Winds of Change vol 1-3

Watch for more at https://www.goodreads.com/author/show/19703964.Angeline_Gallant.

Table of Contents

MARY SAMPSON[1]

Mary passed away in 1816.
A church was built over her grave.

THOMAS SAMPSON[2]

Thomas passed away in 1822.
A church was built over his grave.

JOHANNA JUSTIN SCHREIBER[3]

Johanna passed away in 1855.
A church was built over her grave.

ENOS SCOFIELD[4]

Enos was buried on December 1, 1809.
A church was built over his grave.

MRS. UNKNOWN SECORD[5]

She was buried on September 23, 1796.
A church was built over her grave.

ELIZABETH SELLERS[6]

Elizabeth was buried on November 6, 1800.
A church was built over her grave.

WILLIAM MERRILL SHANNON[7]

William passed away in 1821.
A church was built over his grave.

JANE SHAW[8]

J ane passed away in 1825.
A church was built over her grave.

LUCY ANN SHAW[9]

Lucy passed away in 1816.
A church was built over her grave.

ROBERT SHAW[10]

R obert passed away in 1819.
A church was built over his grave.

WILLIAM SHAW[11]

William passed away in 1813.
A church was built over his grave.

MARY ANN SHEPPARD[12]

Mary Ann was buried on September 16, 1803. A church was built over her grave.

JOHN SHERIDEN[13]

John was buried on February 15, 1810.
A church was built over his grave.

GEORGE SHERWOOD[14]

George passed away in 1819.
A church was built over his grave.

MRS. SARAH SHORT[15]

Sarah passed away in 1815.
A church was built over her grave.

JAMES SIMPSON[16]

J ames was born in May 1816.

He was two years old when he passed away on July 3, 1818.

MARY SIMPSON[17]

Mary was three years old when she was buried on March 28, 1811.

THOMAS SIMPSON[18]

Thomas was born in 1792.

He was 40 years old when he passed away on January 18, 1832.

UNKNOWN SIMS[19]

"Old Mr. Sims" passed away in 1822. A church was built over his grave.

SOLOMAN SKRIMMER[20]

S olomon was buried on August 30, 1799.
A church was built over his grave.

UNKNOWN SMITH[21]

They were only a child when they passed away in 1817. A church was built over their grave.

AMY SMITH[22]

A my passed away in 1817.
A church was built over her grave.

ANN SMITH[23]

Ann was born in 1773.

She was 73 years old when she passed away on April 12, 1846 in Toronto, Ontario. Ann was buried in Kingston.

ANNE SMITH[24]

Anne was born in 1802.

She was a year old when she passed away on September 7, 1803.

ANNE SMITH[25]

Anne was born in 1805.

She was 20 years old when she passed away on May 11, 1825. She is buried with her sister, Anne who passed away when she was a year old.

CHRISTIAN SMITH[26]

Christian was buried on July 20, 1808.
A church was built over his grave.

CHRISTOPHER W. SMITH[27]

Christopher was born in August 1816.

He was 17 years old when he passed away on December 2, 1833. His grave is located beneath the parish hall.

CPT. GEORGE SMITH[28]

George was 80 years old when he passed away on February 26, 1855.

GEORGE BARTLETT SMITH[29]

G eorge passed away in 1816.
A church was built over his grave.

JAMES SMITH[30]

James was born in 1756.

He was 33 years old when the first parliament of Upper Canada assembled on September 17, 1791.

James was 55 years old when he passed away on January 11, 1813.

MARY SMITH[31]

Mary was born in 1774.

She was two years old when New York became the 11th state in 1776.

Mary was 80 years old when she passed away on August 8, 1854.

MARY SMITH[32]

Mary passed away in 1816.
A church was built over her grave.

PETER SMITH[33]

Peter was born in 1752.

He was 39 years old when the first parliament of Upper Canada assembled on September 17, 1791.

Peter was 51 years old when his daughter, Anne, passed away in 1803.

He was 73 years old when his next daughter, Anne, passed away in 1825.

Peter was 74 years old when he passed away on August 15, 1826.

STEPHEN SMITH[34]

S tephen passed away in 1813.
A church was built over his grave.

THOMAS SMITH[35]

Thomas passed away in 1812.
A church was built over his grave.

WILLIAM SMITH[36]

William was born in June 1837.

He was two months old when he passed away on August 18, 1837.

William was buried with his brother, Christopher. A church was built over their grave which is located beneath the parish hall.

WILLIAM SMITH[37]

William was born in 1798.

He was 35 years old when he passed away on July 8, 1833.

GEORGE SMYTH[38]

George was buried on April 21, 1811.
A church was built over his grave.

JANE STUART SMYTH[39]

Jane was born in 1811. She was christened on August 19th.

She was less than a year old when her brother, George Ramsey, passed away in April 1811. Jane passed away five months later in September. She was buried on September 27th.

A church was built over her grave.

KIRBY SMYTH[40]

Kirby was christened on May 18, 1810.

He was less than a year old when his siblings, Jane Stuart and George Ramsey, passed away in 1811.

Kirby was two years old when he was buried on March 10, 1813. A church was built over his grave.

PATRICK SMYTH[41]

Patrick was born in 1783.

He was eight years old when the first parliament of Upper Canada assembled on September 17, 1791.

Patrick was 21 years old when his father passed away in 1804.

Ann and Patrick were married on June 16, 1806 in Kingston, Frontenac, Upper Canada, British Colonial America. He was 23 years old.

Patrick was 25 years old when the Atlantic slave trade was abolished in 1808.

He was 28 years old when his son, George Ramsey, passed away in April 1811. His daughter, Jane Stuart, passed away a few months later in September.

Patrick was 29 years old when the War of 1812 took place.

He was 30 years old when his son, Kirby, passed away in 1813.

Patrick was 32 years old when his sister, Harriet, passed away in 1815.

He was 36 years old when his sister, Rachel, passed away in 1819.

Patrick was 37 when his sister, Elizabeth, passed away in 1820,

He was the founder and first president of the Commercial Bank of Upper Canada.

Patrick ws 40 years old when he passed away in 1823.

JOHN SNARLS[42]

John served in the 41st Regiment.

He was buried on April 29, 1808. A church was built over his grave.

WILLIAM HENRY SPALSBURY[43]

William passed away in 1817.
A church was built over his grave.

UNKNOWN SPARHAM[44]

They were a child when they were buried on September 27, 1807. A church was built over the grave.

DR. THOMAS SPARHAM[45]

Thomas was one of the first settlers in Kingston, Frontenac, Upper Canada, British Colonial America.

He passed away on February 19, 1813. A church was built over his grave.

FRANCIS BROCKHILL SPILSBURY[46]

Francis was christened on December 9, 1761 in London, England.
He was three years old when his brother, Edgar, passed away in 1765.

Francis was eight years old when the Boston Tea Party took place in 1770.

He was 12 years old when his mother passed away in 1774.

Francis was 31 years old when his father passed away in 1793.

He was a surgeon.

Francis was 61 years old when he passed away on August 9, 1823. A church was built over his grave.

CATHERINE SPRATT[47]

Catherine passed away on August 16, 1819. A church was built over her grave.

MICHAEL SPRATT[48]

Michael was born in 1823.

He was a year old when he passed away on July 28, 1824. A church was built over his grave.

UNKNOWN ST. JOHN[49]

She was the wife of the cooper.

She was buried on December 23, 1793. A church was built over her grave.

UNKNOWN ST. THOMAS[50]

He was a sailor when he was buried on April 25, 1793. A church was built over his grave.

JOHN STAUBER[51]

John was buried on March 6, 1805.
A church was built over his grave.

MARY ANN STAUNTON[52]

Mary Ann was buried on May 13, 1810.
A church was built over her grave.

JOHN STEVENS[53]

J ohn was buried on January 5, 1792.
A church was built over his grave.

MARY STEVENS[54]

Mary was buried on January 5, 1792. A church was built over her grave.

NICHOLAS STONEY[55]

Nicholas was buried on April 16, 1798.
A church was built over his grave.

SARAH (OLIVER) STRANGE[56]

S arah was born in 1809.

She was 21 years old when she passed away on June 29, 1830 after giving birth to her first child.

Sarah was buried with her father. A church was built over their grave.

DANIEL STRETCH[57]

D aniel was buried on October 19, 1797.
A church was built over his grave.

THOMAS STRICKLAND[58]

Thomas passed away in 1815.
A church was built over his grave.

ANN ELLICE (ROBISON) STUART[59]

Ann was born in 1785.

She was 27 years old when the War of 1812 took place.

Ann was 31 years old when she married Rev. George O'Kill Stuart, Archdeacon, in Portland, Maine in 1816. She was his second wife.

She was 71 years old when she passed away on November 28, 1856.

CHARLES STUART JR.[60]

Charles was born on November 20, 1814 in Adolphustown, Ontario.

He was less than a year old when his mother passed away in 1815.

Charles was two years old when his father passed away in 1816.

He was a registrar of the county of Frontenac.

Charles was 35 years old when he passed away on April 7, 1850.

SIR. CHARLES STUART[61]

Charles was born on March 31, 1782.

He was a year old when his sister, Mary, passed away in 1783.

Charles was eight years old when the first parliament of Upper Canada assembled on September 17, 1791.

He was 23 years old when he married Mary Ross on May 18, 1805 in Kingston, Frontenac, Upper Canada, British Colonial America.

Charles was 25 years old when the Atlantic slave trade was abolished in 1808.

He was 29 years old when his father passed away in 1811.

Charles was 30 years old when his sister, Mary, passed away in 1812.

He was 32 years old when his wife passed away in 1815. His sister, Jane, passed away on March 15th.

Charles was 34 years old and a sheriff when he passed away on December 26, 1816.

REV. GEORGE O'KILL STUART[62]

George was born on June 29, 1776 in Fort Hunter, New York. He was seven years old when his sister, Mary, passed away in 1783.

George was nine years old when the Shays' Rebellion took place in 1786.

He was 27 years old when he married Lucy Brooks in October 1803.

George was 29 years old when his son, John Brooks, passed away in 1805.

He was 35 years old when his father passed away in 1811 and when the War of 1812 took place.

Charles was 36 years old when his daughter, Lucy Jane, passed away on October 12, 1812. His sister, Mary, passed away a few days later on October 25th. His wife, Lucy, passed away in 1813, before Charles' 37th birthday.

He was 37 years old when his daughter, Lucy Ann Brooks, passed away in 1814.

George was 40 years old when he married Ann Ellice on September 24, 1816 in Portland, Maine. His brother, Charles, passed away a few months later on December 26th.

He was 44 years old when his mother passed away in 1821.

George was 52 years old when his brother, John, passed away in 1829.

He was 56 years old when The Factory Act was passed in 1833.

George was 57 years old when his son, John Brooks Stuart, passed away in 1834.

He was 63 years old when his brother, Andrew, passed away in 1840.

George was 75 when his sister, Jane, passed away in 1852.

He was 77 when his brother, Sir. James Stuart, passed away in 1853.

George was 79 when his brother, Isaac, passed away in 1855.

He was 80 years old when his wife, Ann, passed away in 1856.

George was 86 years old when he passed away on October 5, 1862. He had been an Archdeacon.

JANE STUART[63]

Jane was born on October 17, 1784 and was christened on October 28th.

She was six years old when the first parliament of Upper Canada assembled on September 17, 1791.

Jane was 26 years old when her father passed away in 1811.

She was 27 years old when the War of 1812 took place.

Jane was 28 years old when her sister, Mary, passed away in 1812.

She was 30 years old when she passed away on March 15, 1815.

JANE (O'KILL) STUART[64]

Jane was born on July 3, 1747 in Philadelphia, Pennsylvania. She was christened on the 31st.

She was nine years old when her father passed away in 1757.

Jane was 11 years old when her brother, George, passed away in 1759.

She was 28 years old when she married John Stuart on October 12, 1775 in Philadelphia.

Jane was 30 years old when her mother passed away in 1777.

She was 36 years old when her daughter, Mary, passed away in 1784.

Jane was 43 years old when the first parliament of Upper Canada assembled on September 17, 1791.

She was 64 years old when her husband passed away in 1811.

Jane was 65 years old when her daughter, Mary, passed away in 1812.

She was 67 years old when her daughter, Jane, passed away in 1815.

Jane was 70 years old when her brother, John, passed away in 1817.

She was 73 years old when she passed away on June 10, 1821.

REV. DR. JOHN STUART[65]

John was born on February 24, 1740 in Harrisburg, Pennsylvania.

He was 32 years old when his mother passed away in 1772.

John was 33 years old when his sisters, Mary and Elizabeth, passed away in 1773.

He was 34 years old when his father passed away in 1774.

John was 35 years old when he married Jane O'Kill in 1775.

He was 43 years old when his daughter, Mary, passed away in 1783.

John was 50 years old when the first parliament of Upper Canada assembled on September 17, 1791.

He was 67 years old when the Atlantic slave trade was abolished in 1808.

John was 71 years old when he passed away on August 15, 1811.

JOHN BROOKS STUART[66]

John was born on June 10, 1809 in York, Ontario and was christened on June 16th.

He was three years old when his sister, Lucy Jane, passed away in 1812 and when his mother passed away in 1813.

John was four years old when his sister, Lucy Ann, passed away in 1814.

He was 23 years old when The Factory Act was passed in 1833.

John was 26 years old when he passed away on August 5, 1835.

LUCY (BROOKS) STUART[67]

Lucy was born on June 16, 1775 in Medford, Massachusetts.

She was 15 years old when her mother passed away in 1791.

Lucy was 28 years old when she married Rev. George O'Kill Stuart in Kingston, Frontenac, Upper Canada, British Colonial America in October 1803.

She was 30 years old when her son, John Brooks, passed away in 1805.

Lucy was 36 years old when the War of 1812 took place.

She was 37 years old when her daughter, Lucy Jane, passed away in 1812.

Lucy was 38 years old when her brother, John, passed away on September 10, 1813. She passed away three months later on December 10th.

LUCY JANE STUART[68]

Lucy was born in 1812.

She was an infant when she passed away in September 1812.

MARY ROSS STUART[69]

Mary was born in 1785.

She was 20 years old when she married Charles on May 18, 1805.

Mary was 30 years old when she passed away on June 27, 1815.

UNKNOWN SWEENEY[70]

He served in the 84th Regiment before he passed away in 1783. A church was built over his grave.

PHILLIP TABBOT[71]

Phillip passed away in 1819.
A church was built over his grave.

JOHN TAFFE[72]

John passed away in 1820.
A church was built over his grave.

ELENOR TALBOT[73]

E lenor passed away in 1819.
   A church was built over her grave.

ROBERT TALBOT[74]

Robert was born in 1778.

He was 65 years old when he passed away on December 11, 1843.

UNKNOWN TAVERNIER[75]

He was a French sailor when he was buried on November 13, 1795.

A church was built over his grave.

JONATHAN TAYLOR[76]

J onathan was buried on May 5, 1803.
A church was built over his grave.

WILLIAM TAYLOR[77]

William was buried on February 8, 1801.
A church was built over his grave.

MARY TEMPLE[78]

Mary passed away in 1819.
A church was built over her grave.

PETER THEHMAR[79]

Peter was buried on March 4, 1809.
A church was built over his grave.

ROBERT THOMAS[80]

Robert passed away in 1817.
A church was built over his grave.

ANN THOMPSON[81]

Ann was buried on January 5, 1792.
A church was built over her grave.

HENRY THOMPSON[82]

Henry passed away in 1825.
A church was built over his grave.

MAXWELL THOMPSON[83]

Maxwell was buried on February 26, 1810.
A church was built over his grave.

ROBERT THOMPSON[84]

R obert was buried on December 19, 1809.
A church was built over his grave.

UNKNOWN THOMPSON[85]

They passed away in 1797.
A church was built over their grave.

ADOLPHUS THOMSON[86]

Adolphus was born in 1830.
He was two days old when he passed away.

ARCHIBALD THOMSON[87]

Archibald was the contracting carpenter for the building of St. George's church in 1792.

He is buried in Kingston, Ontario and that church was built over his grave.

ELIZABETH (SPAFFORD) THOMSON[88]

Elizabeth was born in 1791.

She was 21 years old when the War of 1812 took place

Elizabeth was 22 years old when she married Hugh Christopher Thomson on September 20, 1813 in Kingston, Frontenac, Upper Canada, British Colonial America.

She was 23 years old when her father passed away in 1814. Elizabeth passed away the same year.

HUGH CHRISTOPHER THOMAS[89] [90]

Hugh was born on August 11, 1791 in Kingston, Frontenac, Upper Canada, British Colonial America.

He was 20 years old when the War of 1812 took place.

Hugh was 22 years old when he married Elizabeth Spafford on September 20, 1813.

He was 23 years old when his wife passed away in 1814.

Hugh was 24 years old when he married Elizabeth Rutton on March 16, 1816 in Adolphustown, Ontario.

He was 25 years old when his mother passed away in 1817.

Hugh ws 27 years old when his father passed away in 1819.

He was 33 years old when his son, William Henry, passed away in 1825.

Hugh was 34 years old when his daughter, Jane McLeod, passed away in 1826.

He was 36 years old when his sister, Mary, passed away in 1827.

Hugh was 42 years old when his son, Reginald Hebert, passed away in 1833. He passed away a few months later on April 23, 1834, the same year as his son and namesake, Hugh Christopher.

REGINALD HERBERT THOMSON[91]

R eginald was born in 1829.
He was four years old when he passed away in 1833.
A church was built over his grave.

WILLIAM HENRY THOMSON[92]

William was born in 1824.

He was a year old when he passed away in 1825. A church was built over his grave.

[1] https://www.wikitree.com/genealogy/Sampson-Family-Tree-5641

[2] https://www.wikitree.com/genealogy/Sampson-Family-Tree-5642

[3] https://www.wikitree.com/genealogy/Schreiber-Family-Tree-1448

[4] https://www.wikitree.com/genealogy/Scofield-Family-Tree-1390

[5] https://www.wikitree.com/genealogy/Unknown-Family-Tree-618550

[6] https://www.wikitree.com/genealogy/Sellers-Family-Tree-4542

[7] https://www.wikitree.com/genealogy/Shannon-Family-Tree-5510

[8] https://www.wikitree.com/genealogy/Shaw-Family-Tree-26186

[9] https://www.wikitree.com/genealogy/Shaw-Family-Tree-26187

[10] https://www.wikitree.com/genealogy/Shaw-Family-Tree-26188

[11] https://www.wikitree.com/genealogy/Shaw-Family-Tree-26189

[12] https://www.wikitree.com/genealogy/Sheppard-Family-Tree-5448

[13] https://www.wikitree.com/genealogy/Sheriden-Family-Tree-20

[14] https://www.wikitree.com/genealogy/Sherwood-Family-Tree-6298

[15] https://www.wikitrcc.com/genealogy/Unknown-Family-Tree-618558

[16] https://www.wikitree.com/genealogy/Simpson-Family-Tree-24242

[17] https://www.wikitree.com/genealogy/Simpson-Family-Tree-24244

[18] https://www.wikitree.com/genealogy/Simpson-Family-Tree-24245

[19] https://www.wikitree.com/genealogy/Sims-Family-Tree-9740

[20] https://www.wikitree.com/genealogy/Skrimmer-Family-Tree-1

[21] https://www.wikitree.com/genealogy/Smith-Family-Tree-285582

[22] https://www.wikitree.com/genealogy/Smith-Family-Tree-285583

[23] https://www.wikitree.com/genealogy/Smith-Family-Tree-285585

[24] https://www.wikitree.com/genealogy/Smith-Family-Tree-285594

[25] https://www.wikitree.com/genealogy/Smith-Family-Tree-285595

[26] https://www.wikitree.com/genealogy/Smith-Family-Tree-285596

[27] https://www.wikitree.com/genealogy/Smith-Family-Tree-285599

[28] https://www.wikitree.com/genealogy/Smith-Family-Tree-285600

[29] https://www.wikitree.com/genealogy/Smith-Family-Tree-285602

[30] https://www.wikitree.com/genealogy/Smith-Family-Tree-285603

[31] https://www.wikitree.com/genealogy/Unknown-Family-Tree-618605

[32] https://www.wikitree.com/genealogy/Smith-Family-Tree-285605

[33] https://www.wikitree.com/genealogy/Smith-Family-Tree-195302

[34] https://www.wikitree.com/genealogy/Smith-Family-Tree-285610

[35] https://www.wikitree.com/genealogy/Smith-Family-Tree-285611

[36] https://www.wikitree.com/genealogy/Smith-Family-Tree-285613

[37] https://www.wikitree.com/genealogy/Smith-Family-Tree-285614

[38] https://www.wikitree.com/genealogy/Smyth-Family-Tree-3930

[39] https://www.wikitree.com/genealogy/Smyth-Family-Tree-3931

[40] https://www.wikitree.com/genealogy/Smyth-Family-Tree-3932

[41] https://www.wikitree.com/genealogy/Smyth-Family-Tree-3933

[42] https://www.wikitree.com/genealogy/Snarls-Family-Tree-1

[43] https://www.wikitree.com/genealogy/Spalsbury-Family-Tree-21

[44] https://www.wikitree.com/genealogy/Sparham-Family-Tree-57

[45] https://www.wikitree.com/genealogy/Sparham-Family-Tree-58

[46] https://www.wikitree.com/genealogy/Spilsbury-Family-Tree-181

[47] https://www.wikitree.com/genealogy/Spratt-Family-Tree-1083

[48] https://www.wikitree.com/genealogy/Spratt-Family-Tree-1084

[49] https://www.wikitree.com/genealogy/Unknown-Family-Tree-618673

[50] https://www.wikitree.com/genealogy/St.%20Thomas-Family-Tree-47

[51] https://www.wikitree.com/genealogy/Stauber-Family-Tree-109

[52] https://www.wikitree.com/genealogy/Staunton-Family-Tree-539

[53] https://www.wikitree.com/genealogy/Stevens-Family-Tree-27116

[54] https://www.wikitree.com/genealogy/Stevens-Family-Tree-27117

[55] https://www.wikitree.com/genealogy/Stoney-Family-Tree-279

[56] https://www.wikitree.com/genealogy/Oliver-Family-Tree-4953

[57] https://www.wikitree.com/genealogy/Stretch-Family-Tree-454

[58] https://www.wikitree.com/genealogy/Strickland-Family-Tree-7391

[59] https://www.wikitree.com/genealogy/Robison-Family-Tree-2637

[60] https://www.wikitree.com/genealogy/Stuart-Family-Tree-6324

[61] https://www.wikitree.com/genealogy/Stuart-Family-Tree-429

[62] https://www.wikitree.com/genealogy/Stuart-Family-Tree-418

[63] https://www.wikitree.com/genealogy/Stuart-Family-Tree-428

[64] https://www.wikitree.com/genealogy/Okill-Family-Tree-1

[65] https://www.wikitree.com/genealogy/Stuart-Family-Tree-417

[66] https://www.wikitree.com/genealogy/Stuart-Family-Tree-8449

[67] https://www.wikitree.com/genealogy/Brooks-Family-Tree-11445

[68] https://www.wikitree.com/genealogy/Stuart-Family-Tree-8451

[69] https://www.wikitree.com/genealogy/Ross-Family-Tree-29620

[70] https://www.wikitree.com/genealogy/Sweeney-Family-Tree-4969

[71] https://www.wikitree.com/genealogy/Tabbot-Family-Tree-2

[72] https://www.wikitree.com/genealogy/Taffe-Family-Tree-79

[73] https://www.wikitree.com/genealogy/Talbot-Family-Tree-5323

[74] https://www.wikitree.com/genealogy/Talbot-Family-Tree-5324

[75] https://www.wikitree.com/genealogy/Tavernier-Family-Tree-109

[76] https://www.wikitree.com/genealogy/Taylor-Family-Tree-91968

[77] https://www.wikitree.com/genealogy/Taylor-Family-Tree-91969

[78] https://www.wikitree.com/genealogy/Temple-Family-Tree-3459

[79] https://www.wikitree.com/genealogy/Thehmar-Family-Tree-1

[80] https://www.wikitree.com/genealogy/Thomas-Family-Tree-60357

[81] https://www.wikitree.com/genealogy/Thompson-Family-Tree-77675

[82] https://www.wikitree.com/genealogy/Thompson-Family-Tree-77676

[83] https://www.wikitree.com/genealogy/Thompson-Family-Tree-77677

[84] https://www.wikitree.com/genealogy/Thompson-Family-Tree-77678

[85] https://www.wikitree.com/genealogy/Thomson-Family-Tree-12997

[86] https://www.wikitree.com/genealogy/Thomson-Family-Tree-2808

[87] https://www.wikitree.com/genealogy/Thomson-Family-Tree-12998

[88] https://www.wikitree.com/genealogy/Spafford-Family-Tree-41

[89] https://www.wikitree.com/genealogy/Thomson-Family-Tree-2769

[90] https://billiongraves.com/grave/Hugh-Christopher-Thomson/69454722

[91] https://www.wikitree.com/genealogy/Thomson-Family-Tree-2807

[92] https://www.wikitree.com/genealogy/Thomson-Family-Tree-2805

Don't miss out!

Visit the website below and you can sign up to receive emails whenever Angeline Gallant publishes a new book. There's no charge and no obligation.

https://books2read.com/r/B-A-QGSI-ZQGBC

BOOKS2READ

Connecting independent readers to independent writers.

Also by Angeline Gallant

A Dragon's Diary
Dreaming of Dragons

Blood and Spirit Saga
The Rising Wind

Calling Her Heart
Whisper of the Heart
Calling Her Heart Volumes 1 & 2: A Small Town Romance
Collection
No Turning Back
Calling Her Heart volumes 3 & 4
Forsake Me Not
Hear My Cry

FORGET ME NOT
Victoria, Ontario's Babies 1894 - 1895

Guardian of the Heart
Fallen Petals

Keeper Of Secrets
A Lady's Secret

Kingston's Love Chronicles
Springtime Promises

Midnight's Awakening
Heart of the Storm
Walking Through The Storm
Walking Through The Storm
Fighting the Storm
Call Me Cursed
Heart of the Storm

Secrets of the Underworld
Deklan's Dragons

Tell My Story Collection
Tell My Story: Germany 1851
Tell My Story: England 1852

Whispers From The Garrison Church

The Dervock Legacy
Echoes of Dervock

The Grave Whisperer
German Prisoners of War in Canada
Cataraqui United Church Cemetery
Whispers of Kingston
Wedding Bells in Kingston, Ontario, Canada 1923
St. Paul's Anglican Churchyard A-B
St. Paul's Anglican Churchyard C-D
St. Paul's Anglican Churchyard E - F
St. Paul's Anglican Churchyard G - H
St. Paul's Anglican Churchyard J - N
St. Paul's Anglican Churchyard O - R
St. Paul's Anglican Churchyard S - T
St. Paul's Anglican Churchyard, Kingston, Ontario T - Z
Small Graveyards & Burial Grounds: Kingston, Ontario, Canada
Cataraqui United Church Cemetery 1
Cataraqui United Church Cemetery 2
Cataraqui United Church Cemetary 3
Cataraqui United Church Cemetery 4
Cataraqui United Church Cemetery 5
Beth Israel Cemetery
Cataraqui United Church Cemetery 6
Beneath the Surface: Echoes from Beth Israel Cemetery
Grave Tales: Discovering the Lives of Beth Israel
Whispers Beneath St. Paul's

The Timeless Veil
Eternal Devotion

The Wolf Whisperer Series
Captured Heart
Fate's Legacy
Mohawk Valley
Cry of a Warrior
Wolf Whisperer volumes 1 & 2
Endless White
The Wolf Whisperer volumes 1 & 2

Timeless
The Time Keeper's Sanctuary

Timeless Whispers of Dervock Saga
Secrets of Dervock

Standalone
Winds of Change vol 1-3

Watch for more at https://www.goodreads.com/author/show/ 19703964.Angeline_Gallant.

www.ingramcontent.com/pod-product-compliance
Lightning Source LLC
Chambersburg PA
CBHW071534150726
48000CB00002B/791